William

CW01433203

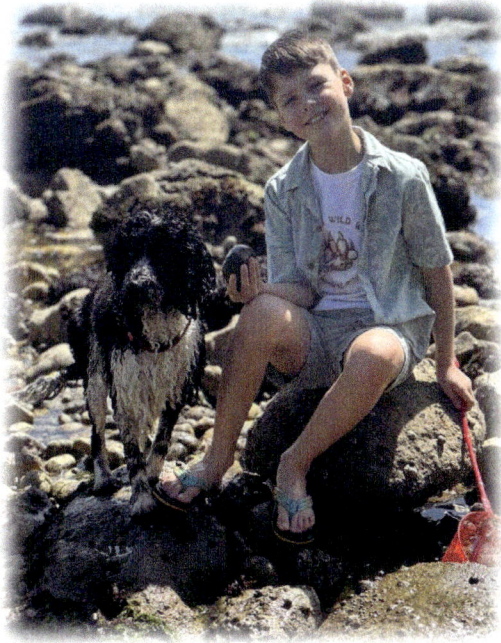

This book is a bucket full of wonder, poured out onto the sand
for anyone who's ever knelt beside a rockpool and whispered,

"I wonder what's in there..."

Welcome to William's Wild World: Secrets of the Seashore

Join me in a magical world just beyond the waves...

Hi there! I'm William, I'm 9 years old, I've got a big brother called George (he's 13 and really good at spotting fast-moving crabs), a cheeky Sproodle called Lola who *loves* the beach even more than I do, and the best Mum and Dad ever, especially when they let us stay out just a bit longer to explore the rockpools at sunset.

If you're anything like me, you probably love running barefoot on the sand, splashing in the shallows, and peeking into those tiny pools of water left behind when the tide goes out.

You never know what you might find hiding there, starfish clinging to rocks, little crabs scuttling sideways, shiny shells with secret stories, or sea slugs that look like something from outer space. It's like the sea leaves us clues to its underwater world... and I'm always ready to go exploring.

In this book, I'll take you with me to my favourite places by the sea.

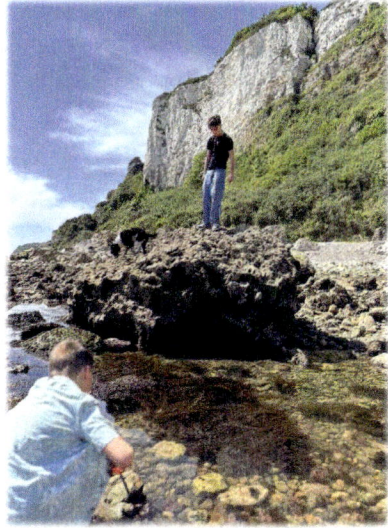

In Lyme Regis and Seaton, on the south coast of England, the rockpools are *full* of surprises. I've found spiky sea urchins, seaweed forests, and even fossilised sea creatures from millions of years ago, it's like nature's time machine!

And when we're lucky enough to be at our other home in Mazarrón, Spain, the warm Mediterranean waters are packed with treasures, too. There are colourful fish, mysterious shells, and creatures I'm still learning the names of.

What makes these places even more special is that I get to explore them with my family. Sometimes George and I turn it into a competition, who can spot the weirdest sea creature, or the biggest crab!

But the best part?

You can become a real-life seaside explorer too.

You don't need fancy gear or a boat, just your eyes, a little bucket, and a sense of adventure.

This book will help you spot amazing creatures, learn fun facts about the animals that live between the land and the sea, and understand how to take care of them, so we leave their homes just as lovely as we found them.

We'll discover:

- How starfish eat (it's *super* weird)
- Why sea snails have such clever shells
- What seaweed is really for
- How to build your own seaside explorer kit
- And how the moon's pull makes the tide come in and out, like magic!

You'll also learn how to explore safely, for you and for the creatures you find.

That means gentle hands, careful footsteps, and always putting things back where you found them. Every rockpool is like a little secret world, and we're lucky guests.

So, whether you live near the sea, visit on holidays, or just *dream* of salty breezes and squishy sand between your toes, this book is for you.

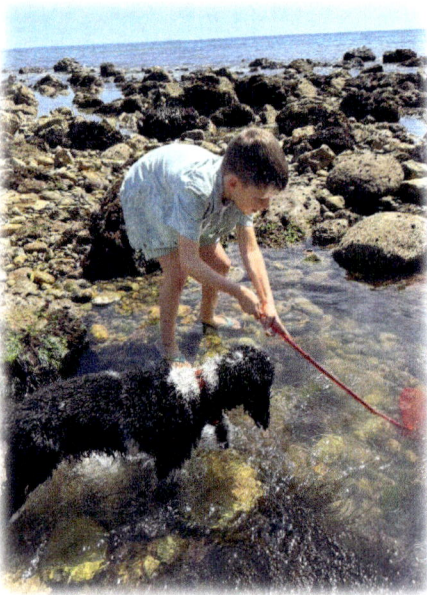

Let's get our feet wet, follow the tide, and discover the secrets of the seashore together.

Ready?

Let's go rock-pooling!!

Contents

The Secret Under the Rock

The sun is shining, the tide is low, and there's only one place I want to be, down by the rocks with my flip flops on and my explorer's bucket in hand.

Lyme Regis and Seaton Hole are my absolute favourite places in the whole world for rock-pooling.

Both on the south coast of England and full of wild and wonderful things, especially when the sea has gone out and left behind hundreds of tiny watery worlds...

ROCKPOOLS!

These shallow pools are like little underwater homes. Some are as big as a bathtub, and others are only the size of a teacup, but if you look closely, they're bursting with life. Seaweed waves like spaghetti, tiny fish dart between stones, and if you're lucky...

you might just find one of my all-time favourite creatures:

A crab!

Meet the Rockpool Crabs

Crabs are the kings and queens of the rockpool. Some are so good at hiding, you'd never spot them unless they move. They come in all different sizes and colours, from tiny green shore crabs to big brown ones with enormous claws!

Most crabs in rockpools are called shore crabs. They have:

- A hard shell (called a carapace) to protect them like a suit of armour
- Ten legs, including two big front claws
- Eyes on stalks, so they can look all around
- And they walk *sideways*! (Why? Because their legs bend that way, it's their crabby superpower!)

Some crabs are bold and scuttle across the bottom of the pool. Others stay very still under rocks or seaweed, blending in perfectly. They're brilliant hiders!

How to Find a Crab (Explorer Style!)

1. Start by crouching down near a rockpool. Stay quiet and still, crabs don't like noisy stomping!

2. Look under seaweed carefully. Crabs love dark places. Gently lift the seaweed and see what's hiding beneath.

3. Check under small rocks. But here's the golden rule: Always lift a rock gently and put it back exactly how you found it. That's someone's home!

4. Found a crab? Yay! Now let's meet it properly...

How to Safely Say Hello to a Crab

Crabs may look tough, but they're actually very delicate. Here's how to make sure everyone stays safe:

- Use your hands like a scoop. Don't grab! Slide your fingers under the crab and gently lift it.
- If you're not sure, use a small net or plastic tub to guide it into your bucket.
- Hold the crab low over the ground or water, just in case it wriggles, that way it won't fall far if it drops.

Explorer tip: Crabs don't want to pinch you. They only use their claws when they feel scared. Be gentle, and they'll feel calm.

Hermit Crab

Giving Your Crab a Comfy Pit Stop

If you'd like to pop your crab into a bucket to look at for a bit, make sure it's safe and comfy:

- Fill the bucket with seawater from the same pool
- Add a bit of seaweed and a small stone or two (crabs like to hide!)
- Keep the bucket in the shade so it doesn't get too hot
- Only keep your crab for a few minutes, then carefully return it to the exact spot you found it

And always remember:

We're guests in their world, it's our job to be polite.

Fun Crab Facts!

- A crab's shell doesn't grow, so it has to shed its shell and grow a new one.
  It's called molting!
- Crabs can regrow a claw or leg if they lose one. Amazing, right?
- Baby crabs are tiny and float around in the sea before they settle into rockpools.
- Crabs "talk" to each other by waving their claws or drumming their feet!

As I gently place my crab friend back into the water and watch it scurry away beneath a rock, I feel a little thrill, because even though I've seen crabs a hundred times before, **each one is special**. That's the magic of rock-pooling, no two adventures are ever the same.

What will we find next?

Grab your bucket, we're just getting started!

Meet the Sea Anemones

After waving goodbye to my crabby new friend, I step carefully over the slippery rocks and peer into another quiet pool. It's calm here, like a secret lagoon where magical sea creatures hide. And right there, stuck to the side of a rock like a bright red jelly button, is something that always makes me grin.

Today the tide's gone out further than usual, and I spot a pool of clear, still water tucked between two big boulders.

As I kneel down and peer in, something catches my eye, a wibbly wobbly blob stuck to a rock. It looks like a squishy jelly sweet, kind of like a gumdrop.

But wait... now it's slowly opening up.

From the middle, soft tentacles begin to unfurl, like petals on a flower stretching in the sun.
This is no sweetie, it's a sea anemone, and it's very much *alive*.

Not a Plant... an Animal!

It might look like a flower, but sea anemones are actually animals, just like jellyfish!
They use their waving tentacles to sting and catch tiny bits of food drifting past in the water.

But don't worry, in the UK, their stingers are only dangerous to things like plankton or tiny shrimp, not to humans. If you gently brush one with your fingertip... it might even squish shut like it's shy!

Weird but true: A sea anemone doesn't have a brain or a heart... but it does have a mouth and a bottom, and they're the same hole. Eww!

Meet the Anemones!

(That's "uh-NEM-uh-nee" — it's a bit of a tongue twister, but super fun to say!)

There are lots of sea anemones in UK rockpools. Here are a few you might spot:

- **Beadlet Anemone** – This is the one I saw! It's usually red or dark green and looks like a blob when the tide's out. But underwater, its tentacles fan out like a pretty flower.

- **Dahlia Anemone** – Much bigger and fluffier! It looks like a colourful pom-pom and can have stripes or spots. They love deeper pools and sheltered rock ledges.

- **Snakelocks Anemone** – Super cool! Long green tentacles with purple tips that wave all the time. They don't hide like others; they love the light.

Anemone Superpowers

Sea anemones might seem gentle, but they've got some amazing abilities:

- They have stinging cells in their tentacles that fire tiny harpoons to catch food

- They stick to rocks with a strong, jelly-like foot called a pedal disc

- If they're in danger, they can close up tight into a squishy ball to hide

- Some can even split in two to make a copy of themselves!

Watching Without Worrying

Anemones are fun to observe, but we need to be careful explorers.

Here's how to enjoy them safely:

Always look, don't poke too hard.
Keep them underwater and never try to pull one off a rock.
If you do touch one, do it with a wet finger so they don't dry out.

Take pictures or draw what you see, they come in amazing colours!

William's Tip: If you find an anemone out of water, don't panic, they're just waiting for the tide to return. They know what they're doing!

Who Lives with the Anemones?

Sometimes you'll find little shrimp or baby fish hiding among anemone tentacles, they get protection from predators there! Some even have a special slime that stops them being stung.

It's like the anemone runs a secret hotel, but only for the guests it trusts.

When they're underwater and happy, they open up their arms like underwater flowers, waving gently in the current.

These arms are called tentacles, and they use them to catch tiny food floating by.

They even have a mouth right in the middle!

Where to Find Them

Sea anemones love to live:

- In shady rockpools
- On the sides of rocks
- Clinging to pebbles or even inside shells

Explorer tip: If the rockpool is calm and clear, you might even spot the tentacles waving like underwater fingers. It's magical.

More Fun Anemone Facts!

- Sea anemones use water pressure to puff up and stretch their tentacles, like a living balloon!
- Some anemones can live for more than 50 years, that's probably older than your mum or dad!
- Baby anemones float around the sea until they find the perfect rock to settle on.

This is why I love rock-pooling.

You never know what you'll find, a crab, a snail, a wobbly anemone… or something you've never even seen before. Every pool is a mini ocean world, full of surprises.

And the best part?

You're part of it when you slow down and take a proper look.

As I sit by the pool, watching the anemone slowly wave its tentacles, I feel like I'm peeking into another world. A slow, quiet world full of secrets, and I'm lucky enough to witness it.

What else is waiting just beneath the surface?

Grab your bucket, we've got a star to find next…

The Star of the Shore – Super Starfish!

If there's one thing that makes me feel like I've found treasure in a rockpool, it's this...
A five-armed, slow-moving, shiny starfish!

I gently move aside the long, slippery fronds of seaweed from the rockpool and *there it is*, shaped like a star, clinging tight to the rock.

A star fish, or sea star!

They're not always easy to find, but when you do, it feels like you've discovered a secret from the bottom of the ocean.
Some are big, with rough bumpy skin, and others are tiny and smooth like wet pebbles. But they all have one thing in common: they look just like stars!

What Is a Starfish, anyway?

You might think a starfish is a fish (it's in the name, right?), but actually, it's not!
Starfish, also called sea stars, don't have fins or gills. Instead, they belong to a group of animals called echinoderms (eh-KY-no-derms), which means "spiny-skinned."

Other echinoderms include sea urchins and sea cucumbers, but let's be honest, the starfish is the coolest.

Amazing Starfish Facts

Most sea stars have five arms, but some have more, up to *forty*!

They don't have a brain, but they do have a mouth underneath and an eye spot at the tip of each arm If one arm gets bitten off... it can grow back!

They eat by pushing their stomach out of their body (yep, really) and enveloping and digesting prey like mussels and clams right inside their shell.

How to Find a Starfish

Starfish are experts at hiding; they don't scuttle around like crabs or flash past like fish. They move very slowly, often sticking tightly to rocks or lying still in a pool of water.

The best way to spot one is to:

- Look in deeper rockpools — especially ones that stay full at low tide
- Check under seaweed or on the side of a large rock
- Look for their distinct star shape, even if they're partly covered in sand or pebbles

Explorer tip: Look underneath a starfish (gently, and only if it's safe) and you'll see its little tube feet wiggling away. They look like rows of tiny suction cups!

Walking or gliding?

When you first see a starfish, it might not look alive, it just sits there. But watch for a moment. You'll see a slow, smooth motion as it moves one arm at a time.

Some starfish have rough, grainy skin. Others feel smoother and softer, like they've been polished by the sea. Just like crabs, if you're going to hold one, you need to be super careful.

Here's how:

- Scoop it gently from underneath with both hands
- Keep it close to the ground or water
- If it's stuck firmly to a rock, don't pull it off. That could hurt its feet!

Kind Explorer Rule: If it doesn't want to come off the rock, that means it's busy doing starfish stuff. Let it be.

A Quiet Moment with a Star

Sometimes, when I sit beside a pool and watch a starfish, it makes me feel calm.
There's something peaceful about the way they move, no rush, no fuss, just gentle exploring.

It reminds me that not all wild things are loud or fast. Some are silent and slow... and that's just as wonderful.

Fun Starfish Facts!

- Starfish don't have bones, they're made of a tough kind of skin with tiny plates inside
- There are over 1,500 kinds of Starfish in the world, but in the UK, you're most likely to find the common starfish or bloody Henry (a red spiny one with a funny name!)
- Starfish are strong! Some can pull open the shell of a mussel with just their arms
- They breathe through tiny gills in their skin

As I gently slide the starfish back into the pool and watch it settle, I wonder what it'll do next. Maybe it'll creep under a rock for a nap. Maybe it's off on a slow, slippery adventure of its own.

Sea Urchins and Strange Surprises

This afternoon, I spotted a cluster of seaweed swaying in a shallow rockpool. It doesn't look like much, but I've learned something on my adventures:

Where there's seaweed... there's treasure.

Then I spot something round and dark, nestled in a crevice.

It looks like a hairy pebble... but it starts to wobble when the water moves.

It's a sea urchin! These spiny creatures might look scary, but they're gentle grazers, not hunters.

Their spines:

- Help them protect themselves from predators
- Let them move slowly by wiggling
- Can even grab things (some sea urchins hold bits of shell for camouflage!)

William's Tip: Be incredibly careful if you pick up a sea urchin, their spines are fragile and can break. If you're not sure, just watch and let them be.

While looking for urchins and sea stars, I spotted these weird and wonderful things too:

Chitons – Tiny oval creatures with armour plates like a medieval knight.

They look a bit like Woodlice but live in the water.

Sea slugs – Colourful, squishy blobs that move super slowly (some look like floating rainbows!)

Sponge colonies – They look like lumps of jelly or strange foam, but they're alive!

Snail Trails and Slippery Shells

As I tiptoe across a patch of soggy seaweed, my eye catches something shiny stuck to a rock.

Not just one, lots of them! Tiny swirls, smooth domes, and some that look like miniature army helmets.
But these aren't just empty treasure finds. These ones are alive, and they're on the move... even if it's super slow!

A World Full of Shells

When we think of the seaside, we often picture colourful shells lying in the sand. But loads of them are actually homes for creatures still inside! From periwinkles to dog whelks, limpets to top shells, each one has its own special way of living on the rocks.

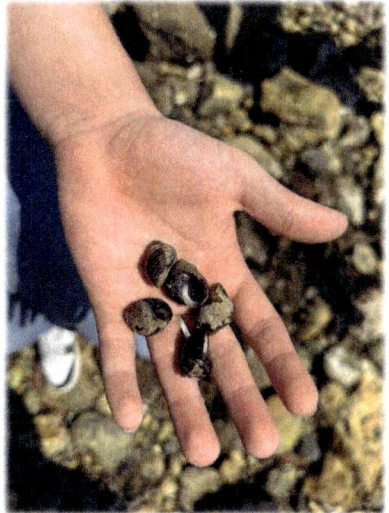

Some crawl around eating algae, others cling on super tightly to avoid getting bashed by the waves. And all of them are part of the beach clean-up crew, keeping things neat and tidy while we explore.

Here are some of my favourite rockpool roamers:

Periwinkles – Little spiral shells that come in brown, grey, or even pink! They slide slowly over rocks munching on algae, leaving behind a shiny slime trail (their version of footprints!).

Dog whelks – Like a pointy periwinkle, but with a powerful trick... they can **drill holes** into other shells to suck out food! Bit gruesome, but hey, it's nature!

Limpets – These guys look like tiny shields stuck to rocks. They never go far and always return to the exact same spot, like their own mini parking space.

Top shells – Like a swirly lollipop shape, these come in lovely colours. You'll spot them climbing seaweed or rocks with a sticky foot and shy feelers.

Shell Creatures Have a Superpower: Their Foot!

Even though they look like slowcoaches, all these creatures have one seriously strong muscle called a foot. It helps them:

- Stick to rocks
- Climb up and down
- Crawl around looking for food
- Hold on tight when the waves crash in

Limpets, especially, are the kings of clinging. You can't pull them off a rock, they create a vacuum, like a suction cup!

Fun Fact: A limpet's foot is so strong that scientists study it to design sticky robots and underwater glue!

How to Spot (and Respect) a Slippery Shell

These shell-dwellers are brilliant to watch, but they're not fans of being poked or picked up. Here's how to be a brilliant beach detective:

- Look for shiny trails or bubbles, that means a snail is nearby!
- If you gently lift one, keep it wet and don't let it dry out in your hand
- Always return it to the same rock or spot you found it
- Don't try to pull limpets off, it can hurt them

Why Shell Creatures Matter

You might think, "They're just snails!" But actually, they're super important to the beach world.

- They keep rocks clean by eating algae
- They're food for birds and fish
- Empty shells become homes for other creatures, like hermit crabs!

After all the excitement of starfish and sea urchins, today feels like a slow, quiet kind of adventure. The tide's going out further, and I spot so many tiny but interesting snails, there's another winkle (it looks like a little curled up snail, but don't tell it I said that!).

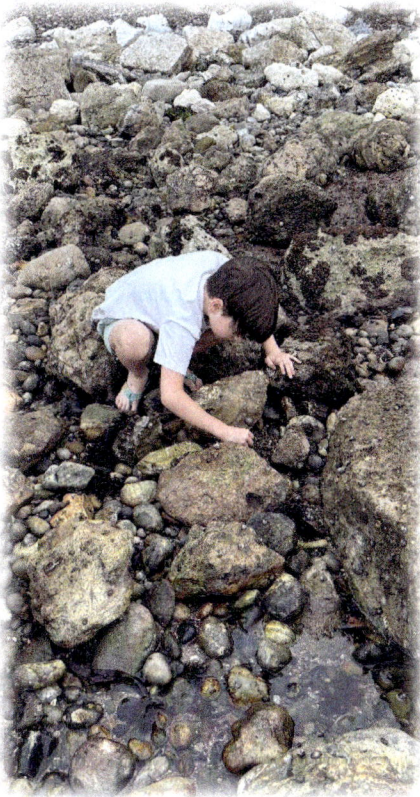

I crouch down to get a closer look. It's sliding slowly across the rock, its foot gliding smoothly, leaving a trail of shiny slime.

So cool!

Winkles: The Little Snails of the Sea

Winkles (also called periwinkles) are sea snails that are so common in UK rockpools. They've got spiral-shaped shells, and their soft bodies are hidden inside, protected from the waves and predators.

There are different types, but the most common ones are:

- **Common winkle** – The smallest, with a **pointed, spiralled shell**

- **Limpet winkle** – A flatter, rounder shell, and they like to live on the edges of rocks

Winkles are great at **clinging tight** to rocks. They use their **foot** (that squishy bit under them) to make a super-strong bond to the surface. Even the strongest waves can't knock them off!

Limpets: The Rock-Suckers

Right next to the winkle, I spot something that looks like a tiny saucer stuck to the rock. This is a limpet, and it's one of the best rock-clingers on the planet.

Limpets have flat, conical shells that look like little cups. They can suction themselves to the rock so tightly that even a hungry seagull can't pry them off!

Here's how limpets work:

- They graze algae and seaweed off the rocks
- They spend all day stuck to their rock, only moving around at night
- They're expert survivors, and their strong foot helps them hold on during the biggest waves

Did you know? Limpets leave behind a shiny trail as they slide along, kind of like their own secret map.

Sea Snails: A Slimey Journey

Sea snails are everywhere in the rockpools, and while they're super slow, they're also really important.

They help keep the rockpool clean by munching on algae, dead fish, and tiny critters. They're like the ocean's little clean-up crew!

A Sneaky Survival Trick

All these slow-moving creatures have a pretty genius survival trick:
They hide when the tide goes out.

When the tide's in, they're safe under the water, but when the water level drops, they stick to the rocks or squeeze into little gaps to stay moist.

William's Tip: If you ever find a sea snail or limpet out of water, be super gentle and place it back in a rockpool to keep it safe!

What I Found Today

Here's what I spotted in the rockpools today:

A winkle with a smooth, spiralled shell
A limpet stuck tight to a rock
A few sea snails munching away on algae
A tiny dog whelk hiding in a little crevice

And the best part? I didn't need to rush or pull things out of the water. I just watched and let them do their thing.

So, every shell you see is either already a home... or about to be one. That's why I always check twice before picking one up.

A Day in the Life of a Snail

Imagine you're a tiny snail on a rock. You wake up, sniff the seaweed, munch on a green snack, then slowly head off for your next snack stop.
Your trail glistens in the sun. A wave washes over your shell and keeps you cool.

At night, you tuck into a crack between the rocks and wait for the tide to return.

It's a small life... but it's full of adventure.

Quick-Shell Quiz!

See if you can spot these while you explore:

A limpet "parking spot" — look for a smooth ring where it always returns
A snail trail — a shiny line across the rock
A shell with bubbles — that means someone's inside!
A cluster of baby snails hiding under seaweed

Tick them off in your journal or draw a sketch!

The waves splash gently against the rocks, and I crouch down to watch a whelk slowly gliding across a pebble. It's not fast, but it's steady, and determined. Just like me on a cold day with a big sandwich.

Ready to meet the next busy beach dwellers?

Let's shuffle over to the rocks and find a spot where the barnacles and mussels have built their own sea city...

Barnacle Builders and Mussel Clusters

Crunch... crunch... **crunch!**

That's the sound my shoes make as I walk across a rocky patch covered in tiny white lumps. They look like someone's glued old popcorn kernels all over the rocks, and they're everywhere!

"Careful where you step," Mum says. "Those are barnacles, and they're alive!"

Barnacles: Tiny Builders of the Sea

At first, I thought barnacles were just boring old bumps, but oh boy, I was wrong.

Barnacles are actually tiny animals that live in cone-shaped shells stuck to rocks, boats, even whales! They're related to crabs and lobsters (even though they don't look it), and they spend most of their lives glued in place.

Here's how they work:

- When the tide comes in, they open up and wave little feathery legs to catch food
- When the tide goes out, they slam their shell shut to stay wet inside
- They build their shells using super-sticky glue that's stronger than anything humans can make!

Weird but true: Barnacle glue works underwater, and scientists are trying to copy it to make sticky bandages for cuts!

What About Mussels?

Right next to the barnacle patches, you'll often find clusters of mussels, shiny, dark blue or black shells all snuggled up together like a crowd of sleepy penguins.

Mussels don't move much either.

They use strong threads, called byssus threads, to anchor themselves to the rocks and each other, forming huge mussel beds.

They're super important because:

- They filter seawater, keeping it clean
- They make hiding spots for baby crabs, snails, and other tiny creatures
- They're a big food source for birds, starfish... and sometimes people (but not from polluted beaches!)

35

A Rocky Seaside City

If you look closely at a big rock at low tide, it's like a mini city:

Barnacles = the apartment blocks
Mussels = the busy marketplaces
Gaps between = dark alleyways full of surprises
Seaweed = the trees
And crabs, shrimps, and snails = the citizens

Every tide brings in fresh water, food, and sometimes even new arrivals!

How to Explore Barnacles and Mussel Beds

This is one of the most exciting parts of a rockpool adventure, but it's also one of the most delicate.

Here's how to explore safely:

- Step carefully, barnacles are sharp and slippery
- Don't pull mussels off rocks, it can damage the whole bed
- Use your eyes more than your hands, look between the gaps to spot creatures hiding underneath
- Look for tiny fish or shrimp darting between the mussels!

Life on the Edge

Living here isn't easy. The creatures that live in mussel beds and barnacle patches have to deal with:

Crashing waves
Hot sun when the tide's out
Cold winds
Hungry birds

But they've adapted in amazing ways. Some close up tight. Others hide deep in the cracks.
It's like they're all saying, "Bring it on, beach!"

Look Closer...

Next time you crouch down by a rock:

Look for tiny white volcano shapes, that's barnacles.
Listen for a faint clicking or crackling sound, that's mussels opening and closing.
Watch for shimmering bubbles, tiny shrimps darting through the rock pools.
Smell the seaweed and salt, that's the scent of rockpool life!

It's not just something to walk past, it's a living, breathing community.

What I Found Today

This morning, I sat by a big mussel bed and counted ten crabs, three shrimp, and a whole bunch of snails hiding between the shells. One even had a tiny sea anemone stuck to its back!

I didn't take anything home, just pictures in my mind and a big grin on my face.

Because the best treasures are the ones you leave behind for someone else to discover.

A Whole Other World

The more I explore, the more I realise this isn't just a beach.
It's a hidden universe, full of tiny aliens clinging to rocks and gliding through the tide pools.

They don't need technology or buildings, their superpowers come from nature.

And they've been living here way before people ever came.

William's Clingy Creature Checklist

Here's what I ticked off today:

Sea star – orange with five arms
Sea urchin – purple, hiding under a ledge
Chiton – tiny but tough!
Sponge – looked like lumpy mustard
Sea slug – like a blob with a party outfit

Next time you're at the beach, try to spot at least one, and remember, take home nothing but photos and stories!

The Mighty Jellyfish and Other Drifters

The sun's starting to set, and I'm sitting on a big rock, watching the water sparkle as it moves in and out with the tide. I'm feeling super lucky to be here. The air smells of salt, and the sound of the waves is like magical music.

But then, something catches my eye.

Floating gently near the water's edge is a strange, almost see-through creature, like a balloon drifting with the current. It looks like something out of a science fiction story, but it's alive.

This is a jellyfish.

Jellyfish are amazing, and they're older than dinosaurs! These squishy creatures have been floating around the oceans for over 500 million years. That's longer than most trees and animals on Earth.

They don't have bones, hearts, or brains, but they've got something even more special, specialized cells that help them move, sting, and catch food.

How Jellyfish Float

Jellyfish don't swim like fish or crabs. Instead, they drift through the water, moving with the currents. They have an umbrella-shaped body called a bell, which they contract and expand, like a jelly-like "pulse." Every time they squeeze their bell, they push water out and zoom forward a little bit.

It's like they're pulsing through the sea!

Weird but true: A jellyfish's body is over 95% water! That's why they're so squishy.

The Tentacle Surprise

Jellyfish have tentacles that trail behind them in the water. These tentacles can be super long and can stretch out even longer than the jellyfish's body.

What's amazing (and a little scary) is that these tentacles have tiny stinging cells called nematocysts. These cells help jellyfish capture their prey, which can be small fish, shrimp, or plankton.

William's Tip: If you see a jellyfish on the beach, don't touch it! Even the ones that seem dead can still sting. Always keep a safe distance and just admire them from afar!

Different Types of Jellyfish

There are lots of different jellyfish, and some are tiny while others are huge. Some of the most common ones you might find on UK beaches are:

- **Lion's Mane Jellyfish** – With long, curly tentacles that can stretch over **30 meters** — that's longer than a **bus**!
- **Moon Jellyfish** – The **classic** jellyfish that looks like a soft, round **moon** with a faint blue or pinkish glow.
- **Barbed Jellyfish** – Known for their sharp tentacles, they like to swim in deeper water, but they can sometimes drift closer to shore.

Why They're So Important

Jellyfish might seem like strange, ghostly creatures, but they play an important role in the ocean. Here's why:

- **Food for Other Animals**: Many creatures, like **turtles** and **fish**, love to eat jellyfish.
- **Part of the Ocean Food Web**: Jellyfish help keep the balance by eating tiny animals like plankton, which are part of the ocean's **food chain**.

- **Soothe the Sea**: Jellyfish actually **clean** the water! By eating small creatures, they help balance the ecosystem by controlling the population of plankton.

While jellyfish are amazing, we do need to be careful. Here are some things to remember:

- **Never touch** a jellyfish, even if it looks like it's washed up on the shore. Their tentacles can sting you, and the sting can hurt!
- If you do get stung, tell an adult right away. You might need vinegar or salt water to clean it and soothe the sting.
- Look out for jellyfish warnings on the beach, some beaches post signs when jellyfish are in the water.

More Drifters: Sea Gooseberries and Comb Jellies

Jellyfish aren't the only drifters you'll find in the sea. There are also some smaller cousins of jellyfish that can be hard to spot but are just as fascinating!

- **Sea Gooseberries** – These look like tiny, glowing jellyfish that are so clear they're almost invisible! They have rows of cilia (tiny hairs) that shimmer in the water.
- **Comb Jellies** – Similar to sea gooseberries, they have rainbow-like iridescent combs that shine like a disco ball when they swim through the water. They move by beating the combs with tiny cilia.

What's Next on Our Journey?

After the jellyfish, I wander a little further along the shoreline, thinking about all the incredible creatures I've seen today. The tide's coming back in, so it's time to head home.

But that's the beauty of rockpooling, no matter where you go, there's always something new waiting to be discovered. Maybe tomorrow, I'll find a strange sea cucumber or a flashy fish hiding under a rock... Who knows?

What Lies Beneath the Waves

Today, the water looks clearer than usual here in Lyme Regis, and I can see the ripples of the waves as they wash gently over the rocks.

I've been rockpooling all day, but now it's time to take my adventure a step further.

I pull off my shoes, roll up my trousers, and wade carefully into the water. The coolness of the sea swirls around my legs, and I feel like I'm entering a whole new world, a world full of hidden creatures and strange underwater wonders.

As I walk through the shallow water, I notice little fast flashes darting past me. These are small fish, swimming gracefully just beneath the surface. They're quick and clever, moving in and out of the kelp and seaweed like they're playing a game of hide-and-seek.

One of my favourite fish to spot is the Rock Goby, the Rockpool Ninja!!

Imagine a tiny fish that's part sneaky spy, part hide-and-seek champion, and totally awesome — that's the rock goby!

This cool little fish lives in rockpools so you might've seen a rock goby zoom away like a flash. Blink and you'll miss it!

It's small (only about the size of your finger!) with smooth skin and colours that blend right in with the rocks and sand. Some are dark brown, others a bit stripey, like they're wearing camouflage. And guess what? They've got two little fins under their belly that stick together like a suction cup, so they can cling to rocks even when the water gets rough!

What Does It Eat?

Rock gobies are always on the hunt for snacks. They eat tiny sea creatures like shrimp, worms, and little bits of whatever's floating by. They're like the vacuum cleaners of the rockpool world, slurp, slurp, gone!

Goby Superpower: Hiding in Plain Sight!

Their best trick?
Blending in!

When a crab or hungry bird comes close, the goby freezes, turns its body just right, and vanishes into the background. It's the ultimate game of "you can't see me!"

So next time you're by the sea and find a little pool between the rocks, look carefully, you might just spot a rock goby ninja watching you back!

Fun Fact: Rock Gobies can *breathe through their skin* a little bit when the water gets low. How wild is that?

William's Tip: Rock Gobies are super fun to watch, but they're also shy, and they bite! If you do try to grab them, be super gentle and very careful!

The deeper I go, the more seaweed I find. These underwater plants might seem like a jungle, but they're a vital part of the ocean ecosystem.

Seaweed comes in all sorts of shapes and sizes, from long, flowing kelp to tiny, leaf-like plants. Some of them are bright green, others are golden brown, and others still are deep purple. It's like a seaweed rainbow!

Underneath the seaweed, I spot creatures that are masters of camouflage, like blennies and wrasse. These fish blend perfectly into the seaweed, making them look like they're part of the plants themselves.

Did you know? Kelp forests (which are big areas of seaweed) are sometimes called the "rainforests of the sea" because they're so full of life and offer shelter to so many creatures.

Blennies: The Rockpool Dwellers

Blennies are small, curious fish with big eyes and funny little fins that make them look like they're always smiling. They love to hide in cracks between rocks and the seaweed, often poking their heads out to see what's going on.

Some blennies have a special trick: they can stick to rocks using their pelvic fins, kind of like how a suction cup works. This helps them stay in place when the waves crash and not get swept away.

William's Tip: Blennies might seem like they're posing for a photo, but they're super quick! So, if you want to get a good look at one, you'll need to be patient and move slowly.

Even though I'm focused on the fish right now, I can't forget about the crabs and other creatures living underneath the water.

Some crabs have special adaptations for underwater life. For example, the rockpool crab is excellent at hiding under seaweed and rocks, while the shore crab is usually found scurrying along the sand or in the shallow waters. I often spot lots of a hermit crabs carrying their little shell on its back as it moves through the water, looking for food.

What Lies Beneath: The Hidden World

What's truly amazing about this underwater world is how many creatures live in such a small space, it's like a whole universe hiding just beneath the waves. I feel like I'm in a secret, magical world where anything could happen!

While the tide is high, I take a moment to stop and look around. The water is filled with life, and it feels like the sea has secrets to tell, secrets that are only revealed if you take the time to look closely.

William's Deep Dive Checklist

Here's a list of what I found today:

Rock Gobies – Little fish that dart in and out of seaweed

Blennies – Curious, smiley fish hiding in rock cracks

Wrasse – Colourful fish that are the ocean's "cleaners"

Hermit crabs – Carrying their homes on their backs

Seaweed forests – A jungle of plants full of surprises

What's Next?

With the tide coming in, I know I have to say goodbye to my underwater adventure, but the sea has already given me so much to think about. I can't wait to come back tomorrow and explore more of this secret world.

Sea Cucumbers, Sponges, and More!

I've had a blast exploring the rockpools and wading through the shallows, but now we're about to dive into an even weirder and squishier world, the deep, dark corners of the ocean floor. Imagine the tide has pulled back even further, and there are parts of the beach even I've never seen before.

It's a bit like stepping into an underwater cave, filled with hidden creatures that don't move around much but are still super important.

Sea Cucumbers: The Slimey Squishies

I squint my eyes and spot something lying on the sand. It looks like a slimy, wriggling cucumber from mum's fridge, but it's not that sort of cucumber at all! This is a sea cucumber.

Sea cucumbers are soft, squishy animals that live on the ocean floor. They're shaped like little tubes, and they move slowly, slithering across the seabed. They have five rows of tiny tube feet that help them crawl, and some of them even look like they're wearing little soft shoes on the end of their bodies.

Weird but cool: Sea cucumbers are detritivores, which means they eat dead things, like fallen bits of algae, shells, and even dead fish. They help clean the sea floor by munching on all the debris!

How Sea Cucumbers Defend Themselves

The best part about sea cucumbers is their amazing defence mechanism. If they feel threatened, some sea cucumbers can spit out their internal organs! These organs get tangled up in the predator's mouth or legs, giving the cucumber a chance to escape.

William's Tip: If you ever see a sea cucumber on the beach, don't touch it too much, it can get very stressed and might even lose its organs!

It's best to just admire them from a distance.

I was forced to very carefully move this little chap as it had been pushed right up the beach and I wanted to make sure it was safe.

Sponges: The Ocean's Cleaners

I keep moving through the shallows, and soon I see a soft, squishy creature sticking to a rock. It's bumpy and looks like a sponge, and that's exactly what it is! Sea sponges are some of the simplest animals on the planet. They don't have legs, heads, or eyes, but they're incredible filters of the sea.

Sponges don't move around much. Instead, they suck in water through tiny pores, filter out the bits of food they need (like plankton), and then push the clean water out again.

They come in all shapes and colours, from round and soft yellow sponges to purple, spiky sponges that look like underwater castles. Some sponges even have holes all over their bodies, making them look like Swiss cheese!

Fun fact: The sponge you use to wash the dishes is actually named after the sea sponge! The real sponges used to be collected from the ocean, but now most are made of synthetic material.

Sea Fans and Coral

As I move further along the beach, I notice soft, feathery creatures growing in the shallow water. They look like underwater trees, swaying gently in the current. These are sea fans, and they're a type of coral.

Coral might look like plants, but it's actually an animal! Sea fans are a kind of soft coral that form branching, fan-like shapes. They're very important to the ocean ecosystem because they provide shelter for tiny fish, crabs, and other creatures. You'll often find them growing in colonies, creating their own miniature forests in the sea.

Cool Fact: Coral, including sea fans, is made up of tiny polyps, small, individual creatures that all live together in a colony.

They're like the building blocks of the reef!

The Underwater Web

As I crouch down and look closer, I start to notice that these creatures aren't alone. There are tiny animals living all around them, tiny shrimp, baby crabs, and even little fish that dart in and out of the soft coral and sponges. It's like an underwater neighbourhood!

Sea cucumbers, sponges, and soft corals all work together in the ecosystem. The sponges and sea fans provide shelter and food for tiny creatures, while the sea cucumbers clean up all the leftover debris from the ocean floor. Everything is connected in this strange, squishy world.

William's Tip: Next time you spot a sponge or sea fan, try to find the tiny creatures living in and around them. You might see baby fish or shrimp hiding in the soft, swaying coral.

What I Found Today

Here's a quick list of my discoveries:

Sea cucumbers — Squishy creatures that clean the ocean floor

Sponges — The ocean's filter machines

Sea fans — Soft, waving corals that provide shelter for tiny sea creatures

Tiny critters — Baby fish, shrimp, and crabs hiding in the soft, swaying sea fans

What's Next?

As I take one last look at the soft sea fans and squishy sea cucumbers, I know I've uncovered some of the ocean's deepest secrets.

The beach might look calm and peaceful on the surface, but under the water, there's a whole world full of action, movement, and strange creatures working together to keep the sea healthy.

I can't wait to come back to explore more with you, maybe next time, we'll discover a sea star hiding under the sand, or spot a crab walking across the ocean floor. There's no end to the discoveries waiting for us!

What happens when the sun goes down and the sea becomes a different world?

In the next chapter, we'll explore the night-time creatures of the ocean, from glowing jellyfish to creatures that only come out after dark!

Creatures of the Twilight Zone

The sun is starting to dip behind the hills, and the beach is quieting down. The air feels cooler now, and I can hear the waves gently lapping at the shore. But as the day fades away, a whole new world begins to awaken.

It's time to go on a night-time adventure and see what creatures come out when the moon rises high and the ocean gets ready for its night shift. With my trusty headlamp on, I'm ready to dive into the twilight zone, the mysterious world where the sea transforms into something magical.

The best part about rockpooling at dusk is that the beach looks completely different in the dark. The soft light from my torch reflects off the water, making everything look sparkly and magical. The creatures that come out at night are much harder to spot during the day, but that's what makes this adventure so exciting.

As I carefully step over the rocks, I spot something floating in the water. It's soft and jelly-like, and when I shine my light on it, it glows! This is a jellyfish, and it's glowing in the dark like a little lantern. Some jellyfish have a special ability to bioluminescence, which means they can make their own light. This glowing is a way to attract prey or to scare away predators.

Jellyfish come in many different shapes and sizes. Some are tiny and float near the surface, while others are big and bell-shaped, with long, flowing tentacles. While jellyfish might look beautiful, they can also sting, so it's important to be careful when you're around them.

William's Tip: If you see a jellyfish at night, look but don't touch! Even if it's glowing, it's still best to admire it from a distance because its tentacles might sting.

Shrimp and Crabs: The Night Crawlers

I'm moving slowly along the rocks, scanning the water, when I notice a quick movement. It's a shrimp, and it's darting in and out of the shadows. Shrimp are much more active at night, and they use the darkness to hide from bigger fish that might try to eat them.

Nearby, I spot a crab scuttling across the sand, its tiny legs moving in a blur. Night-time is when many crabs come out to look for food. They use their sharp pincers to grab at algae, small fish, and even other crabs. Some crabs are really good at hiding, so I have to keep my eyes peeled to catch a glimpse of them.

William's Tip: When you spot a crab at night, it's usually a good idea to let it be. Crabs are nocturnal, meaning they're more active in the dark, so they're likely on a mission to find food.

Sea Stars: The Ocean's Hidden Hunters

I'm kneeling by the water's edge when I notice something slowly moving across the rocks. At first, I think it's a rock, but as I get closer, I realize it's a sea star!

Sea stars, as we know from earlier in our book, are also known as starfish, they're predators, and they love to hunt for mussels, clams, and other shellfish at night. They don't have eyes, but they can sense light and changes in the environment. They move by using hundreds of tiny tube feet, and they can be surprisingly fast when they want to be!

One of the coolest things about sea stars is how they eat. They turn their stomachs inside out to digest their food, which is a bit gross but super interesting!

Did you know? If a sea star loses an arm, it can grow a new one! That's like a superpower for the sea star!

The Ghostly Moon Snails

As I'm walking along, I spot something white, gliding smoothly across the sand. It's a moon snail, a soft, ghostly-looking creature with a spiral-shaped shell. These snails are out and about at night, hunting for clams and mussels to eat. They have a special organ called a "radula," which is like a tooth-covered tongue that helps them drill through shells.

Moon snails are fast movers for snails, and they're really good at digging. If you're lucky enough to spot one, you might even see it burying itself in the sand when it's done hunting.

Sea Snail Supervillains!

Forget what you think you know about snails being slow and boring, these sea snails are **sneaky hunters** with **super skills**!

Necklace Shell – The Driller of Doom!

Name: Necklace Shell
Scientific name: *Euspira catena*

Meet the **necklace shell**, a small sea snail that
lives down on the **lower
shore** (that's the part of
the beach that only
shows up when the tide
goes way out). It may
look harmless, but it's
actually a **meat-eater** —
a carnivore!

This snail loves to eat little clams and bivalves like
Mussels, Scallops and Clams.
But how does it get inside those hard shells? With
its special superpower: **a drilling tongue!**

Yup, it has a radula, a tongue covered in tiny
teeth, that it uses like a mini drill to bore a perfect
little hole right through the shell. Then it slurps up
the soft animal inside like a milkshake.

Brutal... but brilliant!

And its name? That comes from its **egg cases**, which look like a tiny sand-coloured necklace left behind in the tide. It's like the snail leaves jewellery on the beach, weird, but kind of cool!

Next..
Lewis's Moon Snail – The Big Boss of the Sand!

Name: Lewis's Moon Snail
Scientific name: *Neverita lewisii*

Now meet the **Lewis's Moon Snail**, the **giant** cousin of the necklace shell! It's a lot bigger and just as sneaky.

This moon snail also hunts clams and bivalves. It glides through the sand with a HUGE soft foot (it's way bigger than its shell!) and uses the same drill-tongue trick to eat its prey.

If you ever find a seashell with a perfect little round hole in it, guess what? A moon snail probably had lunch there!

Lewis's Moon Snails live deeper down in the ocean, but sometimes they show up in tidepools or shallow sand when the tide is low. If you spot one, lucky you! They're big, blobby, and kind of adorable in a monstrous way!

Fun Snail Facts!

- They're called **moon snails** because of their round, moon-like shells.
- Both snails bury themselves in the sand to **ambush** their prey!
- The holes they drill are so perfect, they almost look like they were made by a tiny laser.

So next time you're on the beach, look for tiny holes in shells or sandy "necklaces." You might just discover the trail of a **moon snail monster!**

William's Tip: If you see a moon snail, look carefully at its shell and try to spot any marks or holes where it's been feeding. It's like a little detective's mystery!

The Ocean's Quiet Night

As the night grows deeper, I take a moment to sit on the rocks with my Dad and listen. The ocean is quieter now, with just the sound of the waves gently lapping the shore. The creatures I've seen tonight are so different from the daytime ones. The night shift in the ocean is full of mystery, glow, and surprise.

It's time for Mum, Dad, George and me to walk up from the beach to our favourite restaurant for dinner after another busy rockpool adventure.

The ocean at night is a whole other world, where everything feels a bit more secretive, and every shadow could hold a new discovery.

Here's what I uncovered during my night-time adventure:

Jellyfish – Glowing, ghostly creatures that light up the sea

Shrimp and crabs – Active and sneaky at night, looking for food

Sea stars – Hidden hunters, slowly moving across the rocks

Moon snails – Ghostly creatures with spiral shells and a taste for clams

As I make my way back along the shore for dinner, the beach feels like it's falling asleep again, and I'm ready for my own rest after such an exciting adventure. But I know that the sea will never stop surprising me. Every time I come here, there's something new to discover, whether it's at night or in the daylight.

Up next, we'll spend another awesome day exploring the smallest of the rockpools, the hidden microhabitats that are home to some of the tiniest creatures in the sea. There's an entire world under every rock!

Creatures That Live in the Littlest Places

You guys know, tidal pools are my favourite places to explore, and I'm about to show you more! These little miniature oceans are scattered all over the beach, hidden between the rocks like tiny treasure chests filled with all sorts of creatures.

When the tide goes out, it leaves behind these puddles of water that are cut off from the rest of the sea. At first glance, they might just look like little pools, but look closer, and you'll see that everything in them is perfectly adapted to live in these tiny, isolated worlds.

From minuscule creatures to colourful critters, tidal pools are teeming with life, and I can't wait to continue showing you around!

71

Let's spend another day together on the beach in Lyme Regis

The first thing I spot today is a tiny crab darting across the pool. It's smaller than the crabs I've seen on the big rocks, and its shell is almost translucent. These little crabs are perfect for tidal pools because they're adapted to hide in the cracks and crevices, where predators can't reach them.

As I lean in closer, I see some baby shrimp, so small they're nearly invisible unless you catch the sunlight just right. These shrimp are incredibly quick and can zip around the pool in the blink of an eye. They're usually filter feeders, which means they're sucking in the tiny particles of food in the water, like plankton and algae.

William's Tip: If you ever want to see a baby shrimp up close, try looking for them in the shallower pools, especially where the water's moving. They're really good at hiding in plain sight, so keep your eyes peeled!

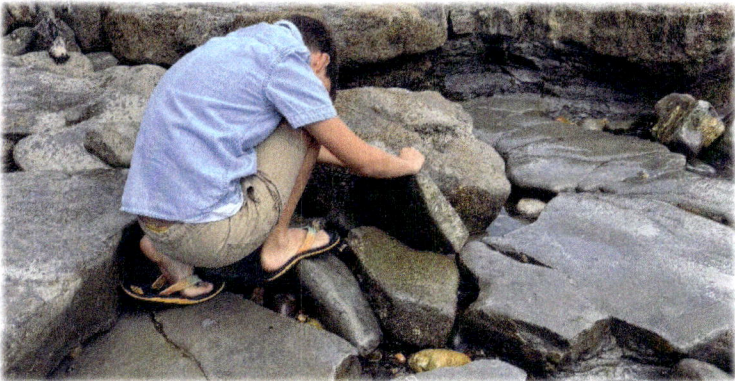

YES! More Flowery Sea Anemones

I notice a soft, wobbly sea anemone swaying gently in the pool. Sea anemones might look like flowers, but they're actually animals! Their tentacles are lined with stinging cells that they use to catch prey, like little fish and shrimp. If you touch one (but be careful!), it will contract quickly and pull its tentacles back in.

Sea anemones come in many different colours, from bright pinks to deep purples, and they can be found tucked into the corners of tidal pools, waiting for a snack to come their way. They're slow-moving, so they rely on the current to bring food right to their doorstep.

More Periwinkles and Limpets

Next, I spot a periwinkle, a small, spiralled shell crawling along the rock. Periwinkles are a type of snail, and they like to stick to the rocks in tidal pools, grazing on algae. They're herbivores, using their little rasp-like tongues (called radulas) to scrape off the algae and eat it. You can find them climbing over rocks and even hiding under the edges to avoid predators.

Not far from the periwinkle, I find a limpet, that small, conical shell that's stuck tight to the rock. Limpets are super strong and use a special foot to hold on to the rock, even when the waves crash in. They might look like they're stuck, but limpets are actually moving slowly along the rock, grazing on algae.

The Secret World Beneath

As I finish exploring, I realise that tidal pools are like little **microcosms**, tiny worlds that are packed with creatures and life.

Some of these creatures are so small you almost need a magnifying glass to see them, but they're all perfectly adapted to live in these little puddles of water. From tiny crabs to colourful anemones, each creature has a special place in the tidal pool world.

What's Next?

As the tide begins to come back in, the tidal pools start to fill with water again.

I take one last look with my rock pooling friends at the tiny creatures that call these pools home, knowing that they'll soon be covered by the sea until the next time I visit. Tidal pools are like secret worlds, and every time I visit, I find something new.

In the next chapter, we're going to talk about diving into the world of shipwrecks and the amazing creatures that live around them.

These underwater wrecks are like sunken cities full of life and mystery. Get ready for an exciting adventure in the depths of the sea!

Shipwreck Adventures in Lyme Bay!

Ahoy there!

Today we're diving (not literally... not yet!) into the incredible tales of real shipwrecks right here in Lyme Bay.

I love looking out at the sea from Beer Head. It looks calm and sparkly now, but it's not always so kind. This bay has swallowed ships like a hungry sea monster, over 200 of them!
Some wrecks are old sailing boats. Some were steamships from world wars. And one HUGE ship, with frozen ducks and perfume inside, ran aground in a giant storm and caused a proper kerfuffle. Let me tell you some of the BEST stories.

The Heroine – Trouble with Sherry and Storms!

Let's start with a wooden sailing ship called The
Heroine (what a great name!).
In 1852, she left the chilly north of England,
heading for faraway Australia with 42 passengers,
tons of barrels of sherry, and lots of dreams.

She sailed into Lyme Bay but things went very,
very wrong. A big storm rolled in, the kind that
makes your hair blow sideways and seagulls
scream. The captain tried hiding in the Torbay, but
another ship was sliding towards them like an out
of control giant.. on ice!

So, to dodge a crash, The Heroine's captain cut the anchor rope and things got worse from there! She smashed into Hopes Nose rock.

Her rudder broke, planks cracked, and the ship was out of control and started taking in water fast. The crew probably pumped like madmen to keep her afloat, but a diver named John Walker later found out the pump had jammed! No wonder she sank.

In Lyme Regis, people woke up to the sound of cannon fire, boom! boom! It was the ship's SOS. Brave townsfolk tried to row out to help, but the sea was fierce. Their little rescue boat flipped, and four of them drowned. It was very sad, but somehow, by the end of the day, all the Heroine's passengers and crew made it to the shore in lifeboats.

The wreck of The Heroine is still out there under the sea, where conger eels now slither between the bricks. (Eww... and awesome.)

Fun Fact: Some of the fire bricks from the ship are still inside the RNLI lifeboat station today, spelling out the word "Heroine" up on the wall! You can see it if you look carefully next time you visit.

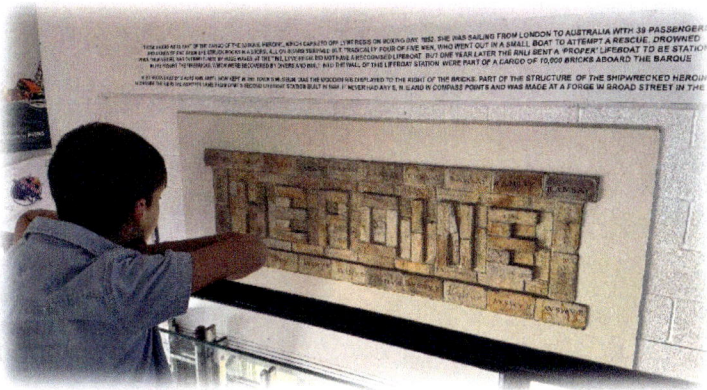

The Baygitano – Boom! A Torpedo in Lyme Bay

Now fast-forward to World War One, when a steamship called the Baygitano (which used to be called *Cayo Gitano*, a bit of a mouthful) was carrying coal across the Channel.

She was steaming nicely across Lyme Bay in 1918 when suddenly – KABOOM!
A German U-boat called UC-77 fired a sneaky torpedo and hit her right behind the engine room.

The ship started sinking fast. Luckily, most of the crew escaped in lifeboats, but two sailors were lost. The Lyme Regis lifeboat, Thomas Masterman Hardy, raced out to help.

It was its very first rescue mission!

Today, the Baygitano lies about 1½ miles south of the Cobb, covered in barnacles and mystery. Divers still explore her today. She's like a giant metal ghost resting on the sea floor.

The Ursa – A Secret Underwater Puzzle

A few months after the Baygitano, another ship met her end in Lyme Bay. She was called the SS Ursa, and she was carrying a whopping 2432 tonnes of coal. That's heavier than a hundred dinosaurs!

She was attacked by another sneaky submarine, UB-104, early one morning. The torpedo hit hold number one (ships have numbered holds like drawers), and she sank in 10 minutes!

The second mate was even taken aboard the submarine for questioning! but was released back to his lifeboat, which was nice of them, I suppose.

Now the Ursa lies way down, 46 metres deep, with her smashed-open bow and spooky-looking galley still visible. Divers love her, but I think I'll stick to rockpooling for now.

The Day the Napoli Crashed Into Branscombe!

This one is bonkers. In 2007, a massive container ship called the MSC Napoli ran into big trouble during a terrible storm in the Channel. She cracked like an Easter egg and was full of weird cargo, dog biscuits, shampoo, perfume, frozen ducks, even BMW motorcycles!

She was too damaged to reach a safe harbour, so the government said, "Okay, beach her in Lyme Bay." So they did. She got stuck off Branscombe beach.

When she started losing containers, hundreds of people rushed to the beach to grab stuff! It was like modern-day treasure hunting.

Some people found wine barrels, others took shoes or even motorbikes still in crates. It got pretty wild.

Just Below the Waves...

So next time you're walking along Branscombe Beach or peering over the side of a fishing boat, remember, deep down under the waves, Lyme Bay is full of sunken ships, forgotten stories, and even lost treasures.

Maybe one day I'll become a diver and visit these wrecks myself. Until then, I'll keep exploring the beach, imagining what lies beneath.

And if you ever hear a strange *clang* underwater? Don't worry, it's probably just an eel making toast with some old fire bricks from The Heroine.

The Lifeboat Station at Lyme Regis

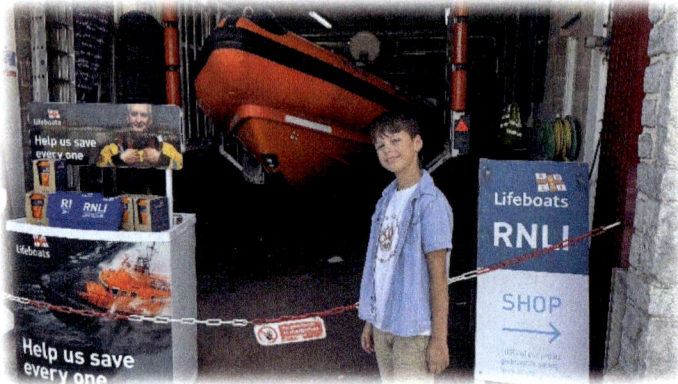

In 1824, a charity was started to help rescue people from shipwrecks. It was called the Royal National Institution for the Preservation of Life from Shipwreck. Today, we know it as the RNLI.

Just two years later, in 1826, Lyme Regis was seen as a place that needed its own lifeboat. This came after a storm in November 1824, when a ship called the *Unity* got into trouble. Local men rescued the crew. Three of them – Captain C. Bennett, William Porter, and John Freeman – were given medals for their bravery. These were some of the first RNLI medals ever awarded.

In 1825, a man named Captain Richard Spencer made changes to a local boat so it could be used as a lifeboat. The RNLI liked what he had done and took charge of rescue work in Lyme Regis from 1826.

From then until 1852, two lifeboats were used, but we don't know their names. On Boxing Day in 1852, as we know, a ship called the *Heroine* was in trouble. It was carrying people to Australia. Five lifeboatmen went out to help, but four of them died. After that, it was clear that Lyme Regis needed a proper lifeboat.

In 1866, the town got its first named lifeboat – the *William Woodcock*. More lifeboats followed:

- *Susan Ashley* (1891)

Thomas Masterman Hardy (1915)

By 1932, the RNLI closed the lifeboat station. New motor lifeboats in nearby towns could reach Lyme Regis faster.

Then, in 1937, the RAF used the beach at Lyme Regis to launch fast rescue boats. This lasted until 1964.

In 1967, the RNLI came back. Thanks to local fundraising, Lyme Regis got a new lifeboat station. Since then, the crew has launched nearly 900 times.

One of the most famous rescues happened in 1979. A yacht called *White Kitten* was stuck in a storm. Four lifeboatmen rescued five people, including a young boy. Two of them were given bronze medals.

The lifeboat used today is called *Pearl of Dorset*. It arrived in 1997. It is faster, stronger, and has better equipment than earlier lifeboats. It can go up to 39 miles per hour and even turn itself upright if it capsizes.

The lifeboat is launched from a trailer pulled by a big tractor. The crew can launch it in just seven minutes. They train and go out on real rescues more than 100 times a year.

Around 36 volunteers help run the lifeboat station. Only two of them are full-time sailors. The rest have other jobs, like teachers, builders, or chefs.

Lyme Regis lifeboat crews have been given many medals for bravery:
1 Gold, 7 Silver, and 3 Bronze.

The RNLI is a charity. It isn't run by the government. It depends on donations from the public. Since it began, the RNLI has saved over 137,000 lives.

William's Tip:
Visit the Lyme Regis Museum to see real artefacts from the wrecks. You might spot a pump from The Heroine or old ship bits that tell tales of the sea. Ask for the sea stories – and say William sent you!

The Mystery of the Wrecks

When you look out at the sea, you might see nothing but water and sky. But under the waves, a whole hidden world exists, full of ancient mysteries and incredible creatures.

One of the coolest, and spookiest parts of the sea is definitely the shipwrecks, the sunken ships that have become underwater treasure troves. These wrecks are not just full of history, they're also full of life. Over time, they've turned into homes for all sorts of ocean creatures, turning a tragic accident into a secret underwater kingdom.

I've always been curious about shipwrecks, where they came from, how they sank, and what's left of them under the water. I imagine them as mysterious ruins, half-hidden beneath the surface of the sea, waiting to tell their stories.

Although I have never visited a real life shipwreck, I still find them fascinating.

The History Beneath the Waves

Some shipwrecks have been lying on the ocean floor for hundreds of years. Others are more recent, but they've all become part of the sea's history. Ships have sunk for many reasons, bad weather, accidents, or even battles. Once they sink, they slowly become part of the underwater ecosystem.

I've heard that around the UK, there are hundreds of shipwrecks just waiting to be discovered! Some wrecks are famous with huge, tragic stories around them, like the Titanic, and others are smaller, more hidden. But each one holds a treasure trove of life, waiting to be explored.

William's Tip: If you're ever lucky, or brave enough to visit a shipwreck (with a safe guide, of course!), look for fish hiding in the shadows. Sometimes they're hard to spot, but if you watch carefully, you might see their eyes peeking out from behind the wreckage.

The Secret Life of the Wrecks

Even though shipwrecks might seem like sad reminders of accidents, they're actually full of life and vibrant ecosystems. They provide shelter and food for so many creatures, from tiny fish to massive octopuses. Every time I think about the creatures living there, I realize that even in places where ships have sunk, nature always finds a way to turn it into something beautiful.

It's like the sea is taking something lost and forgotten and turning it into a new beginning, creating a world of adventure and discovery under the waves.

What's Next?

I can almost imagine myself and George swimming away from a ship wreck, I would have to take a deep breath, feeling so lucky to have explored such a mysterious place.

The sea has so much to offer and explore, and there are plenty of shipwrecks waiting to be discovered. Every wreck has its own story, and I can't wait to uncover more secrets the ocean is hiding.

Time Travel at the Beach

Have you ever wished you could travel back in time and see dinosaurs roaming the earth, or swim with prehistoric fish?

Well, guess what?

You don't need a time machine to do that, all you have to do is visit the beach!

When I'm at my favourite spot in Lyme Regis, I love hunting for fossils, ancient clues to life that lived millions of years ago. Fossils are the remains or impressions of plants, animals, or other living things that were once here, long before any of us. And Lyme Regis is famous for having some of the oldest and best-preserved fossils in the world.

So, grab your bucket, your magnifying glass, and your best detective skills. We're about to travel through time and discover what amazing fossils are hidden in the rocks!

What Are Fossils?

Fossils are like nature's time capsules. They're the preserved remains or traces of ancient living things that lived on Earth long before humans even existed. Fossils can be anything from plant imprints, to bones, to shells that have been turned into stone over time.

When a living creature dies, its body might get buried by sand or mud. Over thousands or millions of years, the soft parts of the creature break down, but the hard parts, like bones, teeth, or shells, can be preserved. Over time, minerals in the ground replace the bones or shells, and they slowly become stone.

This process is called fossilization, and it happens so slowly that the creatures and plants are preserved for millions of years!

Lyme Regis: A Fossil Hunter's Dream

If you're lucky enough to visit Lyme Regis, you're in one of the best places in the world for fossil hunting!

Lyme Regis is part of the Jurassic Coast, a UNESCO World Heritage site. This special coastline stretches for miles and is famous for its ancient rocks that are full of fossils from the time of the dinosaurs.

The cliffs around Lyme Regis are made of rock layers that were once the sea floor, so when you explore the beach, you're walking over ancient oceans, forests, and jungles that existed millions of years ago.

The fossils found here are from creatures that lived during the Triassic, Jurassic, and Cretaceous periods, which makes Lyme Regis an absolute goldmine for fossil hunters like me!

How to Tell a Fossil from a Stone

It can be tricky at first to tell a fossil from an ordinary stone, but there are a few things to look for:

1. Shape and Texture

Fossils often have distinctive shapes, like shells, teeth, or even plant leaves. Some fossils look like rocks at first, but when you look closely, you can spot patterns or textures that are not found in regular stones.

2. Ridges and Patterns

Look for ridges or spirals, those are often signs of something like an ammonite shell. Ammonites are extinct sea creatures with beautiful spiral-shaped shells. If you see a stone that looks like a swirly snail shell, it might be a fossil!

3. Different Colours

Sometimes fossils can be a little different in colour from the surrounding stones. If you find a piece that looks a little darker or lighter, it could be a fossilized bone or a piece of wood turned to stone.

4. Impressions

Some fossils are imprints of the creatures that once lived there. You might find an imprint of a leaf, a footprint, or even a small fish. These impressions are made when the creature gets buried, and the soft parts decay away, leaving behind the shape of what was once there.

Who Was Mary Anning?

Lyme Regis isn't just famous for its fossils, it's also famous for one of the most important fossil hunters in history — **Mary Anning**!

Mary Anning was an extraordinary woman who lived in Lyme Regis in the early 1800s. She was born in 1799 and spent her life searching the beaches for fossils.

One of her most famous discoveries was the first complete skeleton of an Ichthyosaurus, a giant prehistoric sea creature.

Mary's discoveries changed the way people understood the ancient world, and she helped shape the study of palaeontology, the study of ancient life.

Although Mary wasn't famous in her time, today she's remembered as one of the greatest fossil hunters who ever lived. Her passion for fossils helped unlock the secrets of the past, and because of her, Lyme Regis is known around the world as a place where anyone can make their own fossil discovery.

George even found a tribute to Mary when he visited the Natural History Museum in London!

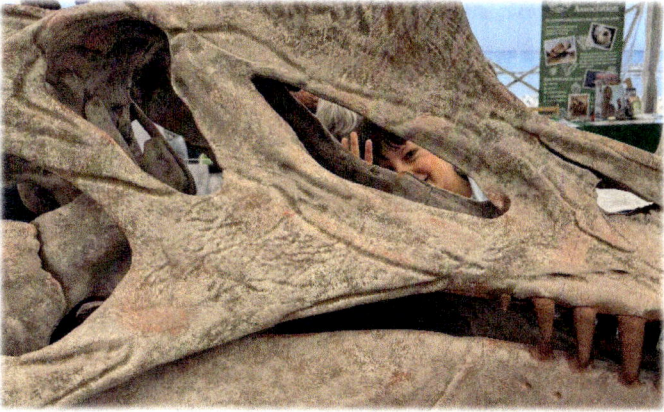

William's Tip: If you ever find a big fossil on the beach, imagine what it must have been like for Mary Anning to make her discoveries all those years ago.

Who knows, maybe you'll find something that's never been discovered before!

Tips on What to Look For

If you're ready to start your own fossil hunt, here are some helpful tips on what to look for:

1. Look at the Layers of Rock

The best fossils are often found in the exposed layers of rock along the beach, especially after a big storm. These layers can be tricky to climb on, so be careful and take your time. Sometimes the fossils are tucked away in cracks or crevices, so keep your eyes peeled!

2. Check the Shingle and Rocks

The tide can wash up fossils onto the shingle (the pebbly beach) as well as along the shore. Look for interesting shapes or imprints in the rocks, and use your magnifying glass to get a closer look at anything that seems unusual.

3. Pay Attention to Fossil "Fossil Beds"

Certain areas of the beach might have fossil beds, places where many fossils are found close together. These areas are usually marked, so make sure you follow the signs and always ask a local guide if you're unsure about where to look.

4. Use Tools (Safely!)

Sometimes, the fossils are hidden deep inside rocks, so it might help to bring a small hammer or chisel. But be very careful when using tools, make sure you're not damaging the fossils or the rock layers they're in.

5. Take Your Time

Fossil hunting isn't about rushing, it's about exploring the hidden history beneath your feet. Take your time, be patient, and you'll be amazed at the tiny fossils that show up when you least expect them!

The Ocean's Changing Rhythm

Have you ever wondered why the sea rises and falls every day, like a giant, breathing creature? It's not just magic, it's the tides, one of nature's most amazing and predictable rhythms. The tides are an important part of life at the beach, and they can help you discover even more about the ocean and its creatures.

I've spent hours watching the tide come in and go out at Lyme Regis, Beer and Seaton, and it's like the sea has its own secret dance that's been going on for millions of years. There's something magical about seeing the tide roll in, covering the beach, and then retreating to reveal hidden treasures, like sea creatures and fossils.

In this chapter, I'll explain how the tides work, why they're so important, and how you can make the most of them on your next beach adventure!

What Are the Tides?

The tides are the regular rising and falling of the sea's water level. This happens twice a day, and it's caused by the gravitational pull of the moon and the sun on Earth's oceans. The moon has the strongest pull, which is why the tides are most noticeable when the moon is closest to the Earth.

As the moon moves across the sky, it creates a bulge in the ocean. This is why the tide rises.

When the moon is on the opposite side of the Earth, another bulge forms, causing the tide to rise there, too. And in between, the water levels fall, that's when you get the low tide!

The sun also has an effect on the tides, but it's not as powerful as the moon. When the moon and sun align (during full moons and new moons), the tides are even higher and lower than usual, these are called spring tides.

When the moon is at a right angle to the sun, the tides are lower, called neap tides.

Why Are the Tides Important for Beach Life?

The tides play a huge role in shaping life at the beach. When the tide comes in, it brings fresh water, nutrients, and food for all sorts of marine creatures. But when the tide goes out, it reveals hidden treasures, things like rockpools, shells, and fossils that were covered by water.

Low tide is the perfect time for exploring. The sea has retreated, leaving behind all sorts of amazing things to discover. You'll find crabs, starfish, and sea anemones in rockpools, and the rocks are often covered with barnacles and seaweed.

But high tide is also important because it brings in new creatures and helps sea creatures that live in deeper waters. Some animals follow the tide as it moves, and the current can carry them from one place to another, bringing new life to the beach.

How to Use the Tides to Plan Your Adventure

One of the best ways to make the most of your beach adventures is to plan them around the tides. If you want to explore rockpools and find the best creatures, you need to know when the tide is low.

You can easily check tide times on a tide table or tide chart. These tell you exactly when the high tide and low tide will happen. If you want to see lots of creatures, aim for a low tide, that's when the rockpools will be the most accessible.

Tip: The best time to go fossil hunting in Lyme Regis is during low tide, when the cliffs are exposed and you can see the rocks more clearly.

What Happens at High Tide?

At high tide, the beach is almost covered by water. This is when the ocean is at its highest point and can come right up to the edge of the cliffs. High tide is great for watching how the sea changes — it's a time when the waves crash against the rocks, and you can see the full force of the ocean.

You might not be able to explore the rockpools during high tide, but you'll find marine life that only comes out when the water is deep. Fish swim closer to shore, and sea birds might be flying over the waves, looking for food. The beach will look completely different, and you'll get to see the powerful rhythm of the sea as it moves in and out.

What Happens at Low Tide?

At low tide, the sea retreats, leaving the beach uncovered. This is the best time for exploration. The rockpools are revealed, and creatures like crabs, shrimp, sea snails, and starfish are easy to find. The rocks and sand are exposed, making it the perfect time for fossil hunting.

During low tide, the seaweed beds are often visible too, and you can learn all about the different types of seaweed and how they provide homes for tiny marine creatures. You might also spot some seashells scattered along the shore.

Tides and Fossil Hunting

Fossil hunting at Lyme Regis is all about timing. If you're hunting for ancient fossils, you'll want to be there at low tide. That's when the sea has pulled back, exposing the cliffs and the layers of Jurassic rock where fossils are often found.

The fossils that are exposed at low tide could be from creatures that lived millions of years ago — long before humans even existed! Look for ammonites, shark teeth, and other ancient sea creatures. Some of the fossils can be found in the rocks, while others are revealed in the shingle (the pebbly beach) as the waves pull back.

William's Tip: Always be careful when hunting for fossils in the cliffs at Lyme Regis. The cliffs can be unstable, and the rocks can sometimes fall. Stick to the safe areas, and don't climb too high up the cliffs.

What's Next?

The tides are always changing, and with every high tide and low tide, a whole new world of discoveries awaits. I love how the sea never stays the same, and each day brings something new.

In the next chapter, we'll explore the powerful forces that shape the sea, from waves to currents.

We'll also dive into how weather and storms can change the beach and bring out new creatures. Get ready for a wild ride with the ocean's mightiest forces!

Waves, Currents, and the Power of the Sea

Have you ever watched the waves crashing against the shore and wondered where they come from? Or felt the pull of the ocean as it drags you back into the sea?

The ocean is one of the most powerful forces in nature, and there's so much more going on beneath the surface than you might think. The waves, the tides, and the currents all work together to shape the beach and create the ever-changing landscape of the coast.

I love watching the waves at Lyme Regis, especially when the tide is high, and the sea looks wild and untamed. The power of the ocean is amazing, and it affects everything from the sand beneath our feet to the animals that live there. In this chapter, I'm going to show you how waves are made, how currents work, and how you can learn about the mighty ocean and its incredible power!

What Are Waves?

Waves are created when wind blows across the surface of the ocean. The wind pushes the water, creating a ripple effect that turns into a wave. The size of the wave depends on how strong the wind is and how far it travels.

When you see big waves crashing on the beach, they've usually come from far out in the ocean, where the wind has been blowing for a long time. The waves get bigger the further they travel, and by the time they reach the shore, they can be huge and powerful.

As the wave gets closer to the beach, it slows down and gets taller, until it breaks and crashes on the shore. This is the wave crash you see when the sea seems to explode with foam. Waves are what make the beach so exciting, but they also play an important role in shaping the coastline by eroding the cliffs and moving sand around.

What Are Ocean Currents?

The ocean is full of currents, huge rivers of water that move through the sea. Unlike waves, which are caused by the wind, currents are caused by a variety of factors, like temperature differences, salinity, and even the Earth's rotation. Currents move water in one direction, and they can travel for thousands of miles across the ocean.

Currents are important because they distribute heat around the Earth and help control the climate. The warm water near the equator travels toward the poles, and the cold water from the poles moves back toward the equator. This movement helps create the ocean conveyor belt, a system that keeps our planet's temperatures balanced.

You might not always see the currents, but they're always there, moving through the sea and affecting everything in their path. Some currents are very strong and can pull objects and creatures along with them. It's important to be careful in the sea because strong currents can be dangerous, especially for swimmers.

The Power of the Ocean

The ocean is powerful, there's no doubt about that! Waves can be strong enough to erode cliffs, wash away sand, and even create new beaches. The sea has been shaping the coastline for millions of years, and it will continue to do so in the future.

But it's not just waves that make the ocean so powerful. The tides, the rise and fall of the water, are driven by the moon's gravity. The force of the tides can move huge amounts of water and can be felt all over the coast.

During storms, the ocean can be at its most powerful, with huge waves and dangerous currents. Storm surges can cause the sea to rise higher than normal, flooding the shore and causing damage to beaches and cliffs.

Even when there isn't a storm, the ocean is constantly changing, with new waves, tides, and currents shaping the coast every day. It's like the sea has its own never-ending rhythm, constantly moving and shifting.

How Waves Shape the Beach

Waves play a big part in creating the landscape of the beach. When waves crash on the shore, they carry sand, pebbles, and other materials with them. Over time, these materials are worn down and broken into smaller pieces. This process is called erosion.

The waves also shape the sand dunes, which are formed by the wind carrying sand from the beach to higher ground. Sand dunes are important because they act like a natural barrier against storms and high tides.

The shape of the beach also changes because of waves. Longshore drift happens when waves push sand along the beach in a zigzag pattern. This can move sand from one part of the beach to another and change the coastline over time.

So, the next time you see the waves, remember: they're not just for surfing or swimming, they're powerful forces that shape the beach and the world around us.

The Ocean's Creatures and the Power of the Sea

The power of the ocean doesn't just affect the land, it also affects the creatures that live in the sea. Animals like crabs, fish, sharks, and whales all rely on the ocean's currents to move around, find food, and even migrate.

Some creatures, like sea turtles, salmon, and whales, travel thousands of miles using the ocean's currents to guide them.

And don't forget about the rockpools, they may seem calm and still, but they are constantly affected by the rise and fall of the tides and the waves that crash on the shore.

The animals that live in rockpools, like sea anemones, crabs, and barnacles, have adapted to live in these changing conditions, and they're tough little survivors.

On my adventure today, I watched the ocean's mighty forces at work

The waves were huge at high tide, crashing against the rocks and creating foamy spray.
I spotted some seals bobbing in the water, riding the currents with ease.
The sand was being moved around by the waves, creating new sandbanks on the beach

I found a starfish clinging tightly to the rocks in the rockpool, using its strong grip to survive the changing tides

What's Next?

The ocean is constantly changing, and every time I visit the beach, I discover something new. The tides, waves, and currents may seem like they're just part of the landscape, but they're a vital part of the rhythm of life on the coast.

As the Sun Sets

The sun is slowly dipping below the horizon, casting golden light across the rooftops of Lyme Regis. The tide has crept back in, gently covering the rockpools that, just a few hours ago, were alive with scuttling crabs, darting fish, and curious explorers with buckets and big smiles.

Down on the beach, the last few footprints are washed away by the waves. Seagulls call to each other in the sky, and a soft breeze carries the salty scent of the sea inland. Another day of adventure is coming to an end.

Up the hill, tucked into a cosy stone cottage with whitewashed walls and a little garden full of daisies, William is home.

His sandy shoes are by the door, his bucket and net are drying on the porch, and Lola, his black and white sproodle, is curled up at his feet, tired from a day of sniffing out seaweed and chasing the tide.

Inside, the fire crackles gently, and Mum is making hot chocolate while Dad and the boys flip through a book about sea creatures. George is sharing tales of the tasty crepes from the shop just off the beach and his favourite salted caramel ice cream.

William, warm and happy, is wrapped in his favourite beach towel, still a little bit salty, still a little bit sandy, but completely content.

He stares out of the window, watching the sky turn pink and orange over the sea. His heart is full of everything he saw today, the dancing shrimp, the hidden starfish, the fossil shaped like a spiral. And his mind?

Well, it's already racing ahead to tomorrow.

Because one thing's for sure, tomorrow will bring another adventure. There are still rockpools to explore, seashells to collect, and stories to discover. There might be new creatures to meet, new secrets hidden beneath the seaweed, and *definitely* a stop for ice cream (maybe even two!).

Having a home by the sea is the best thing in the world. And for a boy like William, every day is a chance to dive into nature, laugh with his family, and learn something amazing about the world around him.

So, if you ever find yourself on the shores of East Devon or Lyme Regis, bucket in hand and eyes scanning the beach for treasure, keep a lookout.

Because William might just be there too, peering into a rockpool with Lola by his side and a smile on his face.

And if you spot him?

Don't forget to say hello.

The Rockpool Explorer's Promise

As the sun begins to dip and the tide rolls back in, our adventure for today comes to an end. But the sea never sleeps, and tomorrow, there will be new creatures to discover, new shells to collect, and new stories to tell.

Being a seaside explorer isn't just about finding cool things, it's about caring for the creatures and their homes. Every crab, snail, seaweed patch, and shiny pebble is part of a much bigger picture. And when we look after nature, we become part of something amazing, too.

So, here's my promise, and maybe you'll say it with me:

I promise to tread lightly,
To explore kindly,
To leave only footprints,
And to always respect the sea.

I'll be curious, careful, and full of wonder,
Because every creature counts,
And every rockpool is a little world of its own.

Thanks for joining me on this seaside adventure. I hope it's only the beginning. Wherever your wild world takes you, keep exploring, keep asking questions, and never stop looking just a little closer. Because that's where the magic is.

Until next time...

Your fellow explorer,
William

Although, before we completely end this adventure I thought I should take you on a short visit to my summer holiday home, we're heading south to Mazarron, Spain, one of my favourite holiday places for exploring the coast.

The warm Mediterranean waters are full of new creatures, and I can't wait to dive into the rockpools there. Get ready for some sun, sand, and sea creatures from a completely different part of the world!

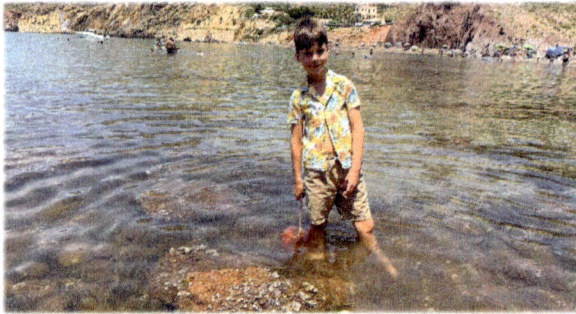

The Warm Waters of Spain

Hola! Welcome to the sunny beaches of **Mazarron and Bolnuevo**, Spain!

If you've ever wanted to explore a beach that feels like summer all year long, then this is the place to be. The Mediterranean Sea is full of exciting creatures and hidden treasures just waiting to be discovered. And the fun part?

It's so different from the beaches of East Devon and Lyme Regis (and much warmer!)

I've been lucky enough to spend lots of time with my family at our second home in southern Spain, and every trip is like stepping into a new world of sea life.

The warm, clear waters are perfect for snorkelling, rockpooling, and even fossil hunting, but there's one big difference, the animals and plants can be so different from what I find back home in the UK!

In this chapter, I'm going to take you on an adventure through the Mazarron beaches, from the calm rockpools to the wild cliffs, and show you the incredible creatures that call this sunny coastline home. So, grab your bucket and spade, we're about to embark on a whole new seaside adventure!

A Beach Like No Other

Mazarron is breathtaking. The beaches here are lined with rocky cliffs, and the water is so clear you can see all the way to the bottom.

The sand is golden, and the weather is sunny almost every day, perfect for exploring!

The coast around Mazarron is special because it has a unique mixture of warm Mediterranean waters and rocky shores. This creates the perfect environment for all kinds of animals, from tiny crabs to big fish.

The warm waters mean there's a whole new set of creatures to discover, many of which you won't find on UK beaches.

Ready to dive in?

Rockpooling in the Warm Waters

When the tide goes out at Mazarron, the rockpools are revealed. But instead of the familiar creatures we see in the UK, the rockpools here are home to Mediterranean creatures. They have adapted to the warmer waters, and they live in different ways compared to the cold-water creatures of the UK.

One of the first things you'll notice are the huge number of sea anemones.

These beautiful creatures come in different shapes and colours, and they love to hide in cracks and crevices. They're like little underwater flowers, swaying with the current.

But be careful, I've learnt very painfully, they can sting, so don't touch them too roughly!

Another exciting find is the Mediterranean crab. Unlike the crabs you might find at home, these crabs are often brightly coloured and more active.

You'll spot them scuttling across the rocks, especially during the day when they're looking for food. They're fast and fun to watch, but just like their British cousins, you should always be gentle when handling them. If you find one, be sure to lift it carefully by the back legs and never try to hold them by the pincers.

And don't forget about the sea snails. The warm waters are full of them, and you'll find them climbing the rocks or hiding under seaweed. Some of them have amazing shells that come in all shapes and sizes, and they're fun to collect (just make sure they're empty before you take them home).

Amazing Underwater Life

If you want to see the true wonders of Mazarron, you've got to get your snorkel on. The waters are incredibly clear, and with a bit of patience, you can see some fantastic underwater life. From schools of small fish darting between rocks to moray eels hiding in crevices, there's always something amazing to spot beneath the surface.

I've had some incredible experiences snorkelling here. One of my favourite finds is the Mediterranean octopus. These clever creatures are experts at camouflaging themselves against the rocks, so you've really got to be on the lookout! If you're lucky, you might even spot one in a rockpool, or see it swimming lazily around the sea floor.

The seagrass meadows around Mazarron are home to a variety of creatures too. These underwater forests are perfect hiding spots for baby fish, sea urchins, and starfish. The seagrass is super important for the ocean, as it provides a home for many animals and helps keep the water clean.

Fossil Hunting by the Cliffs

Bolnuevo and Mazarron are famous for more than just its beaches and rockpools. The cliffs and rocks here are rich in fossils, and if you know where to look, you can find some amazing ancient remains. While the Jurassic Coast in Lyme Regis is famous for its prehistoric past, the cliffs of Mazarron have their own history to tell.

The cliffs are full of marine fossils, like shells, corals, and even fossilized fish. You can sometimes find ammonites and sea urchins, just like the ones I discovered in Lyme Regis, except these ones are from the Miocene period, which is much younger than the ancient rocks of the UK.

To find fossils, you'll need to look at the layers of rock along the cliffs. The sandstone and limestone here often hold imprints of long-gone creatures. As the weather erodes the rock, new fossils can be exposed. But be careful! The cliffs can be crumbly, so always stay safe and make sure you're not climbing too high.

The Wonders of the Mediterranean Sea

One of the coolest things about being in Mazarron is the chance to explore an entirely different ecosystem. The warm waters of the Mediterranean are home to many unique creatures that you won't find in the colder waters of the UK. Here, you might even spot sea turtles gliding by, or see dolphins leaping in the distance.

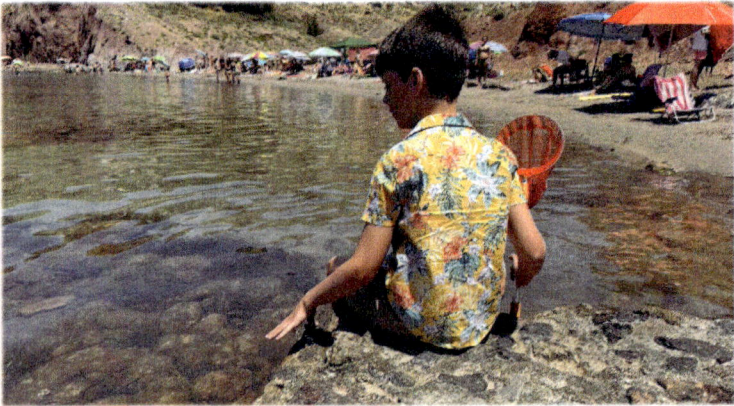

The seabirds in Mazarron are also fascinating. You'll spot gulls, herons, and even flocks of migratory birds that stop at the beach to rest. The rocks and cliffs make perfect places for birds to build their nests, and you can watch them swooping down to catch fish from the sea.

On my adventure today, I discovered:

A super fast Octopus he didn't want to be caught!

A sea snail with a beautiful spiral shell

A school of small fish swimming around a patch of seagrass

A giant sea anemone, waving in the current

A fossilized sea urchin in the cliffs, almost perfectly preserved!

What's Next?

Mazarron and Bolnuevo have shown me that every beach is different, and each one holds its own secret world of creatures. From rockpools to warm seas, there's always something new to discover. And even though the beaches of the Mediterranean are quite different from the ones in the UK, one thing is the same: there's always an adventure waiting around the corner.

Bonus Pages & Activities

Seashore Scavenger Hunt

Can you spot all of these on your next beach trip? Tick them off as you go!

- ☐ A crab hiding under a rock
- ☐ A shell that spirals
- ☐ A patch of wobbly seaweed
- ☐ A rock with holes in it (who made those?)
- ☐ A tiny fish in a pool
- ☐ Two different kinds of sea snail
- ☐ A smooth, flat pebble
- ☐ Something that's not natural (and should be picked up!)

Explorer tip: Don't forget to look gently under seaweed and always put rocks back where you found them!

Rockpool Spotter's Guide

1. Shore Crab – Green or brown with big pincers. They scuttle sideways and love to hide!
2. Limpet – Like a tiny volcano stuck to rocks. Super strong suction powers!
3. Sea Anemone – Looks like a flower but it's an animal. Its tentacles wave gently in the water.
4. Periwinkle Snail – Small, spiral-shelled snail that climbs rocks.
5. Starfish – Has five arms and can regrow them!
6. Blenny Fish – A slippery, wiggly fish that hides in seaweed.
7. Hermit Crab – Lives in other creatures' old shells — and swaps when it grows.
8. Barnacle – Tiny volcano-shaped animals stuck to rocks. They open when wet!

Did You Know? Barnacles are related to crabs — even though they look nothing like them!

Make Your Own Rockpool Journal

You should start your own story, just like mine!
In you journal make sure you list things like:

- **Date of visit**
- **Where you went**
- **What you saw**
- **What the tide was like**
- **Drawings of your best finds**
- **One special moment to remember**

William, and Lola love nothing more than
updating their journal with all of the rockpool
finds.

Printed in Dunstable, United Kingdom